T0158326

The Ohio State University Press/ *The Journal* Award in Poetry

Empire Burlesque

Mark Svenvold

THE OHIO STATE UNIVERSITY PRESS • COLUMBUS

Library of Congress Cataloging-in-Publication Data
Svenvold, Mark, 1958–
 Empire burlesque / Mark Svenvold.
   p. cm. — (Ohio State University Press/ *The Journal* Award in Poetry)
  ISBN-13: 978-0-8142-5166-9 (pbk. : alk. paper)
  ISBN-10: 0-8142-5166-8 (pbk. : alk. paper)
  I. Title.
  PS3569.V48E47 2007
  811'.54—dc22
                                    2007023073

This book is available in the following editions:
Paper (978-0-8142-5166-9)
CD-ROM (978-0-8142-9155-9)

Cover design by Jason Gray
Type design and typesetting by Juliet Williams
Type set in Adobe Garamond
Printed by Thomson-Shore, Inc.

The paper used in this publication meets the minimum requirements of the American
National Standard for Information Sciences—Permanence of Paper for Printed Library
Materials. ANSI Z39.48-1992.

9 8 7 6 5 4 3 2 1

For Ron Wandover, wherever you are

Contents

Part Three: Let Nothing You Dismay

Part Four: News to Pluto

Acknowledgments

Grateful acknowledgement is made to these publications, where the following poems, under slightly different titles, first appeared:

Agni Review: Jeffersonian

Barrow Street Review: Sacagawea Somniloquy

The Death of the Cabaret Hegel (Chapbook): To an Unknown Poet, Dead at 39

The Frost-Proof Review: Landscape With Man, Ax; Memo: from the Manitou, 1804; Memo: As the State of Mind in Which We Are Generally Gives the Colouring to Events; The Past as Obsolete Gesture

The Iowa Review: Memo: Understanding As I Do That This Little Work Would Be Nothing In Itself.

The Journal: Avaunt & etc; Memo: From the Platte; Memo: To the Assembled Corps; Celestial; Shannon, Lost; VII (When does it begin, this blurring into error?); VIII (Evening evolves a salad of shadows); Upper Missouri: In Search of the Shoshone; Shannon, Found; Lochsa River Apology; Our Story (So Far) as the Function f(x); Charon Crossing, Mississippi

Ploughshares: The White Pages; I'd Really Rather Be in Authentic City

Poetry 180: Pre-Amputee to Reviewers

Swink: Minimalism (Kong, After *Empire,* by Andy Warhol)

The University of North Texas Press: Empire Burlesque, From *Soul Data,* by Mark Svenvold. © 1998.

Memo: Understanding As I Do That This Little Work Would Be Nothing In Itself, Lacking Authority, Unless It Were Favored And Protected By A Person Whose Authority Would Protect It From The Boldness Of Those Who, Without Reverence, Give Their Murmuring Tongues Liberty, And Knowing As I Do How Great Are The Obligations Under Which I Have Always Been, & Am

—*Arkansas River, 1543*

The real trouble, seen in hindsight—
that Don Antonio de Mendoza,
farther than ever from his beloved sardine *tapas,*

could not keep position, nor govern well, alas,
and with Cortez out there, somewhere, and coming on—
the pressing question, amid the sage and chaparral,

the sun-cracked earth, and those coughing, dusty tribes
awaiting miracles, the real question, for a diarist
and observer of this empty-headed spectacle of blood,

it seems, was what to do with the assembled gentlemen-dandies
shipped off by their fathers for great *obras*—
Pedro de Guevara, son of Don Juan de Guevara,

nephew of the Count of Oñate, &c and for instance,
whose *cabeza* they found particularly *vaca,*
blinking into the tarnished squalor of another sunset—

Don Lope de Urrea, laughing at his own jokes,
Francisco Gorbalan, the Unaccommodating,
so called, Don Alonso Manrique de la Otiose,

also known as "Little Fatty," and Paco the Offbeat,
who later shot himself in the eye—
What captaincies would you give the likes of these?

◄◈►

As for Coronado? One followed him
and that was that. One did not question
certain things, even as the days amassed,

even as the land began its tricks,
—*why not drop that sea chest, anyway?*
and their methods of inquiry grew less

—how shall we say—*diplomatic?*
O moon, O horizon of staggered
double amputees, wonder of wonders

to thread atrocity through the narrowing eye
of the historical method. Shall we lie down, instead,
& sleep all winter? For they were terrifying, yes,

and also a bit ridiculous. (The local's early best defense:
to nod & point them farther on).

       —One did not question
even as the spell of the sky fell hard upon them,
how under that sky,

the land beneath like a treading mill
or some great, scrolling script beneath them,
held them fixed in its vastness,

though if one stopped in the dust
and let the horses pass, until the glitter
of helmets and the shouts of the goatherds

vanished like bells into the processional wind,
then, it seemed, a former world,
in one sweeping view, realigned itself in the heart.

The past behind, the future ahead, in clinking armor.

And here, within that part of the past,
amid the swell
of sweet grass, chest-high, under a sky
and the sky's trance, which says, *a little farther on,*
I have made this hasty note:

> the grassland opens like a sea
> and then, like a sea,
>   closes behind.

ONE
Plus Ultra

Jeffersonian

Because it was, and because it was enough,
it seems, so that: yonder star-swirl might compose
but the smallest flower or leaf thereof,
and in that leaf a world . . . because He chose,
for He was busy—what with mollusk and mountain,
because it all fit—weasel, flea, and spore,
because the difficult, the unforgiving forms
of continental granite and jenny wren
brooked no counter, no other, no outer, no ex,
posed no irony of scillia, no pause, supposed
no sad planet afloat in oceanic space,
no lone and troubled inheritor-savant,
—because they lived unpredicated, reader,
like a sand fly or a sea cliff or a river . . .

◄◆►

II

They brought oilskin bags for their journals,

they brought instruments:
two sextants,
a horizon,
a sun,

artificially its term and angle
reflecting in a pan,

and other gear to measure
the land,
the river's reach, its extent—

you will notice and comment on the soil,
the date at which particular plants
put forth or lose their leaf, or flower;
times of appearance of particular birds,

reptiles, insects . . .
dinosaur bones,
volcanoes. . . .

—◄◊►—

(which would require, at the very least, it seems,
something to write with)

six papers of ink powder, crayons, and sets of pencils

    (and something to write on)
        field tables,
(and something to see with at night)
          twenty gross of candles
    (and something to keep out the weather)

    sheets of oiled linen for tents and sails
       six large needles, six dozen awls
  (and for warmth) six dozen woolen pants,

   30 yards of common flannel, one hundred flints,
   30 steels for striking or making fire—

    . . . because they could & because it was there,

and, since it was in St. Louis, 1803—
    that Auguste Chouteau
and all the fine girls and buckish Gentlemen,
danced as they danced as they danced
      to celebrate Napoleon's
Garage Sale—

  they brought a surveyor's pole & chain,
      and a set of plotting instruments—
         (Meanwhile. . . .

◄◊►

. . . . Up river, the Sioux:
hostile, numerous, well armed,
certain to demand ransom for passage)

Hence: Guns & Ammo, Mail Order Dept—

one swivel-mounted cannon made of bronze,
four heavy shotguns or blunderbusses,
four hundred pounds of lead for shot
fifteen Pennsylvania rifles,
two hundred pounds imported rifle powder.

(and a little something for insects & etc.)
a mosquito net,
curtains; 8ps cat gut,
two hundred pounds
of tallow mixed with fifty pounds of lard
which they smeared

"about the arms & face
to repel the most pugnacious"

mesquetor . . .

misquitr,

muscatoes. . . .

◄◈►

They brought the new Jerusalem,
and the firepower to back it up;

They brought the God of Joseph Mede
"Awakened out of sleep."

His tools and *His* fondness for gadgetry—
an air rifle, a collapsable
"semicylindrical," iron frame canoe.

and from Thomas Parker of South Third Street, Philadelphia,
a very expensive watch—

"with her a screw-driver and kee,
the works stoped by inscerting a hog's bristle"—

They brought fifteen pounds of Peruvian bark,
for malaria,
they brought books—

two volumes of Linnaeus, Barton's *Elements of Botany*

The Nautical Almanac and Astronomical Ephemeris—

(and something out of Locke and something out of Bacon
and something out of Newton—
for instance, the medicine of one Dr. Rush)

to wit:

◄◈►

III

When you feel the least indisposition,
do not overcome it by marching.
Rest in a horizontal position.

Benjamin Rush, that is, whose pills
"cure all of mankind's ills"—

To be your own best physician,
take these pills for a general purging.
When you feel an indisposition,
                              —*calomel,*
six parts mercury to one part chlorine—
            called "Thunderclappers" by name.

. . . an attack of fever? of ague? Just listen—
for what I've said bears repeating—
If you assume a horizontal position,

and opium, and niter or saltpeter, and jalap,
            and whiskey and a little laudanum

. . . soon all will be well again.
You won't hear your men complaining,
anyhow, of the least indisposition.

For they've brought presents
for all the new tenants
            ten pounds assorted sewing thread;
            silk fabric, and paint, and vermillion—

and they'll be more refreshed, I say, by *lying down.*
That's key. Prevent verticality. No leaning,
no listing, no half-hearted *horizontalisme*

                        should be allowed. In sum: go prone
                        briefly, it goes without saying,
                        and, at the least indisposition—
                        be sure to rest in a horizontal position.

IV

They arrive
like emperors of China, recognizing no equals
                              only tributaries,

with 12 dozen flags,
and 12 dozen friendship coins,
and whiskey by the barrel,

   the ocean breaks its shackles
        and a great earth lies open—

   the stone rolls down the mountain
   and the rivers run backward
       and a new generation ascends
in a keelboat, in canoes,

with small cheap scissors,
and common brass thimbles,
and 288 knives; and combs;

  and *Kirwian's Elements of Minerology,*

  and *A Practical Introduction to Spherics and Nautical Astronomy*

   and ear trinkets, and arm bands,

    and red glass beads
    and white glass beads
    and blue glass beads

  tunc Orientis occidit et ortum est . . .
      . . . imperium sine fine dedi.

TWO

Landscape with Man, Ax

I

Exeunt

Being as it was October on the Plains,
the mammals gathered into their herds—
elk, pronghorn, buffalo, and squirrel
especially, and in such numbers they'd sound
from a distance, like a sleek, chittering river
moving through the overstory of oak and hickory
until they reached the banks of the Missouri,
where they'd pause, as Meriwether reports,
"and with lusty abandon, plunge into the waters."
A flock of pigeons flew above us, blocking the sun.
Making haste, I set up my espontoon & let loose
with the blunderbus. The birds, en masse,
shat upon us, and those I struck dropped
by the dozen like tennis balls upon our decks.

II
Memo: from the Platte

Farther, further untethered from Western Civ.,
(while you were out)—the advance men cometh,
a bunch of guys ahunting. The prairie giveth
of venison and buffalo, the steak, tongue & humps of,
and they taketh notes beneath the big star-sieve:
Caught 500 catfish near the river mouth. . . . &c.
Tonight, despite Linnaeus, they'll hear the prairie wolf
carry the river, the trees, the very bluffs above,
and think on Magick and other strange business
seen & unseen. They keep their muskets primed,
and stand by the sentry fire, listening & alert,
startled now and then, perhaps, by the soft, page-rustle
                                          of oblivion—
as the flicker of some long-extinguished star
plays upon the field its million-millionth part.

III

Voyager, 1804

N. 23, W. 7½ Ms. a pt. L. S. psd. Mon. [Manitou.] Creek

Sore-eyed from sand and river glint,
a thunderhead off the bow, Labiche dreams
of Truffles Morella, how she'd stand for him

come spring, in nothing but her hat and boots,
as it seems she does now, high aloft, in curls
that disembogue along her ample curves,

comme ça? and frisks his shirt again—
It's enough to stop a young man's heart.

And as a dream carries its own momentum,
its own pitch and timbre, into a wilderness
busy with birdsong and death, so

his line of sight like some surveyor's chain
against the river's argument, propels him
now, with us implied, in tow.

IV
Memo: To the Assembled Company

Up and down the river, in weather foul or fair,
in a keelboat, in canoes, westward to the ocean—
Did I mention we'll be rowing there?

Rowing, pushing, hauling from the shore,
in brush and biting flies, like plodding oxen,
up and down the river, in weather foul or fair?

Did I say that we'll be famous, we'll get a share
of land, of women, a book deal, a movie option?
Did I mention we'll be rowing there

a quarter ton of lead and rifle powder,
flags, whiskey, a pair of mounted cannon
up and down the river, in weather foul or fair?

And for the locals, Dr. Rush's questionnaire:
When do you dine? What about baths? Depression?
Your oracles—Did they mention we'd be rowing here?

Do we seem to bristle? Excuse us—for we're
a blessed, bristling nation. Please excuse the renovation
up and down the river, in weather foul or fair.
—Did I mention we'd be rowing there?

Memo: As The State Of Mind In Which We Are, Generally, Gives The Colouring To Events, When The Imagination Is Suffered To Wander Into Futurity

[Ft. Mandan, Winter, 1805]

So, thence—

into the matter, shag ice on the water
rimed around the boats, which sink.

thus: onto & plunging through it,
poking at the problem with a stick,
men chopping away knee deep in the slurry
while at their backs
the great sideways-blowing, always oncoming

wind

siege-like, abiding in the dark
beyond the parapets, in which
no country, no philosophy, no emissary
or allegiance, no god liveth

unless it be by the flicker of tallow candles
(Clark at his maps)
or in a blacksmith's sense of providence—
(Joe Shields, US Army)
at his coke hole of charred pitch pine
forge fuel, covered with dirt,
against wind-flare, or "God's bellows."

He tends the smoking pile, while others
intermingle with the Big Bellies
a few squabbles already abrew—

(Some little Miss understanding
thro jelloucy

so that Cruzat is sent (again) with his fiddle
and York with his *physique extraordinaire*
to wow 'em in their huts, &c. . . .)

Meanwhile, the sergeant knows a proper smolder,
banked down, will warm the winter,
& prove up the morning we wake, cold & hungry
and find him,
banging out sheet-iron for village corn.

—◅◇▻—

—*a verry Cold frostbitten morning*
                the Sun Shows—

mutatis mutandis—two images
floating in the atmosphere, rainbows
hover mandala-like over the *ménage à corps*—
                so cold one man
                complains his pecker froze,

another's arse needs
                defrosting in a water tub—
Another spends Christmastide with a fever
while those more merrily disposed
                fire guns & cannon,
& head for a frolic with the village women:

which commences, come evening,
                with the calling of the Buffaloes—

—*First, tawny damsels offer themselves*—

a sort of boy scout's wet dream
                (for quick reference, Lads!
c.f. Moulton, pg 90; Bergon, Penguin edition, pg 84,

the operative part, *in flagrante*
                found also in Biddle's latin translatio)—

—next the wife, with the spreading of her body
          rekindles the old man—

multum ille jactatus est
          (but enfeebled by age, it seems)
               frustra jactatus est,

though in this way,
of course, all manner of things derive:

—the white men with their shining mirrors
like solid water held in the hand
               brilliant as the sun
& which sometimes show their faces—

& shows even now, down the city boulevards,
          with the traffic's ebb and flow
down the Avenue of the Americas,
the sun-torched flare,
          that blinds us,
          of an afternoon,
—that swept them like a prairie fire.

A Crossing

From them the dust and from them the storm,
and the smoke in the sky, and a rumble in the ground;
and from them the very sky seeming, from afar, parabolic;
from the curve or girth beyond the eye's reach;

        from/across/& through—

a beautifull level and fertile plain—
with soggy bottoms of slender allium
or nodding onion the size of a musket ball,
white, crisp, well-flavored; from the high grass stretching

        into tomorrow

the welcoming committee assembles & gathers—
each dark visage a massive escarpment
that stares out of bewilderment;
—from their river crossing, and from somewhere

        inside the huff, hieratic ohm—

the beck-and-echo, returning call
of calves mothering-up; from the dark script
of the herd, frequently *approaching more nearly*
to discover what we are,
        with/across/& to

the cataract of time:

this steady, animal regard,
this gaze of theirs, the size and scale of it,
so amassed,
arrests the men, who look them back

        as they must /& do/& will—

from a bookcase, from a window sill.

Untoward Memo

How best extract wonder from tedium,
clear shaft of light from shuffling
discourse on Mule deer,
Elk vs. Antelope, & etc,

the city's on-going marginalia
like soft snow settling upon the kingdom of the unread,
someone polishing the library's tiled floor
all afternoon with one of those big, circular-ish
floor buffing thingys—outside,
mid-week, trash swirling at one's feet?

Wade patiently,

leave amorous note
for hot librarian.

The Bitterroot

Fr. *Racine amère,* or (lit.) *root bitter;* always the French
preceding them with a toe hold in the tongue,
so to speak, the lingo (Sioux, Shoshone) they've come
so far to sway away, to wow, to woo.

Drouillard drops a sack of roots,
(fusiform, abt six inches long, rind white, thin)
& new to science from some fellow stole his gun,
his first mistake, then fled (his second) to the bench

above river, D in hot pursuit, &c. The issue
quickly settled—no dead—*hoi physikoi* set to
(cilindric, hard, size of a small quill)
which, on a smoky fire they bring to boil

& nearly gag on. Later, a quiet brand of misery,
like embracing a bayonet, each to his own.

Sacagawea Somniloquy

Her story, and the story's custodians—
I mean historians—
      are all abed.
Earlier, they'd shared
a last glass of Chardonnay over the waters,
while a sunset the color of orange highlighter
underscored whatever it was the horizon
and one or two seabirds were trying to say.
            Later, maybe more than a few
paired up for some quiet talk,
overheard by the wave wash and the gossip
of blown spartina grass. What happened then
is anyone's guess: awkward moments
for which no amount of sophistication
prepares us—and we're not talking *ultra*
sophisticates here, we're talking tweedy
scholars making exceptions for themselves,
angling for a bit of recompense,
sweet fever in a librarian's ear,
the double bed in the hotel room
like the tidal pull of a big cliché.

      That part of history
we'll never know. Off duty, the custodians
dream a voluptuous, antiquarian sleep
in which the shelves begin the murmur and call

across cross references,
disciplines & distances—

It's then the moon summons her story—
the moon, untitled, unsponsored, free.

V
Celestial

Full dark, and in the cooling night air
the scent of dog tooth violet and mayapple,
and the burgeoning suck and slide of the river
boiling with unseen cargo, the freighted tangle
of toppled, up-ended things borne away:
trees, animals, the dreams of exhausted men.
Colter snores. Drouillard and sergeant Ordway
share a nightmare, a boat tossed on its beam-end,
the deck vertical . . . Meanwhile, beyond the trees,
Meriwether shoots the stars, or rather, sights
the moon's slow wade and toggle against Anatares,
calling out the numbers to Captain Clark—
and regular as clockwork, Clark complies,
records, by lantern light, the unencumbered skies.

VI
Shannon, Lost

—all manner of shouting in the wilderness—
some calling out, some signal shots fired,
someone sent off—Colter or Droulliard,
some reliable one, who will return,
empty-handed, muttering into his shirt,
punk kid, or some lost version thereof.
The boats advance, and Shannon, too, advances,
closing a gap, following a line of thought,
skirting overland, his eye to the water,
or down to and across the water,
chest deep, the line with horse in tow
slicing through tansy and willow
like straight talk through fancy speech—
always ahead, always a little farther on.

VII

When does it begin, this blurring into error?
Floribunda fabulosa, the sun's tip-and-run
westward in the overstory—nightfall soon,
and then what? Wind in the trees, a little thunder . . .
What's the last thing you remember?
a ridgetop, a shifty sky that said, either/or,
some slight delay forever lost to us, Shannon,
now reduced to this: a guess—upstream?
down?—and you get it wrong. Well then,
with no end to starting, the days amass
and burn against the chestnut-colored hills.
By night you shiver, thinking you've been passed.
At dawn you precede a reputation, which grows
against you & gets slight mention in the journals.

VIII

Evening evolves a salad of shadows—
the river darkens and spools an atmosphere,
a dim seep into rocky shallows,
a lacquered sky the river mirrors.
Upriver, "out," a full week of nights
hiding under a leaf, unable to hit
a deer not even if she stroll right up & beg
Here Shoot Me, George, but it's no use no good
So: he picks grapes, wonders wherefore
(&c)—eats and picks & eats & shits grapes.
You see there's very little romance in it
when you know—as you know one or two things, ever
like a truth-hollow in the gut. Then, it's best to wait
by a riverbank & aim to set things straight.

IX
Upper Missouri: In Search of the Shoshone

The vanishing act continues. Clear sign:
a prairie fire in the distance, a shadow path
for ghosts called an "Indian road" by some,
which dissolves (again) into a dead-end swath
of sedge, of bulrush and blue flies—another nowhere.
Well, *that's* a bit glum. Expecting trouble,
see, is what makes a Meriwether have all
seven of the seven habits of highly effective people.
Still, the men work by day, shiver by night—
asleep as soon as they drop, with snowfall soon,
thunder and hail now, and Shannon lost.
"Lest any accedent should befall me," Lewis writes,
dryly hedging his bets, and names a successor:
—the night wind shifts, as if to answer.

X
Shannon, Found

You rise at dawn from your bed of boughs
tensed and blinking from a dream that ended
with a snap of—what?—a branch? . . . your senses
whip-ready, primed by the slightest noise—
You watch for a figure, but nothing shows . . .
In that decisive moment, let's say you've heard
the chip of a grackle in the click of a cocking-piece,
and you relax your guard. If you're a moose,
you're dead. If you're a man, you've been had again,
and still you can't see him. You'll call out, "Colter?"
He'll smile, and then, like a Cheshire in reverse,
(though here I've got my history wrong), he'll appear
without a word, for he'll have said it all
in shades, in limbs of beech & buckskin, teeth first.

XI
Lochsa River Apology

"Reduced in circumstance," Clark reports,
"we suped on skant soup, a little bear oil
& twenty pounds of candles" melted for tallow.
As they pass, ridge upon ridge, the Bitterroots
cast and recast the terms of next resort,
(for there cannot, there will not be, a last).
And hunger makes the best of bootlace al
dente, for instance: picante, but as tough to swallow,
perhaps, as this coarse meandering from fact.
Sorry. I'd mend my ways, but the fact is
the river undercuts, frustrates and beguiles
the plan, theirs and mine, the crow's route
we hunger after. And the river offers no other
method, which is why they call them river miles.

XII
Our Story (So Far) As The Function *f(x)*

It is the part of a slippery variable
to stand for something other: a nest of eels,
for instance, or the smell of a man in fever.

If the smell of a man in fever,
and the square root of all the blisters
on all the hands that carry us in this, our sedan,

were stitched together some rain-besotted day,
it would make a rather smallish jib for the furthering,
yet how very like a variable to carry that sail

and the storm itself, and the bitter current
by moonlight, river mist ghosting
along a line's chop and heave.

And if, as is our wont, we keep falling for it,
for the part where the empathy runs—
some poet kneeling to light candles

to our patron saint of the crescendo—
well, the wily variable can carry that, too,
in a sorry sort of road-house,

rain along the Natches Trace, a summons
to the Capital, Meriwether with a pistol to his head. . . .
Ever the volunteer, he steps

into the unsayable. You wanted some drama, didn't you?
to be and to get carried away, as they say?
It is in keeping that a pattern should so

ramify & thus bewilder, in keeping that a pattern,
through which we move & are moving, should end,
and that an ending be its forwarding address.

Coda: The Past as Obsolete Gesture

—Marianne Moore, Cumberland County, PA, 1903

And from the great Return (shift) spool-
ing (tab) of paper, from a clamor on the plattens,
from a better time and place to put the hyphens,
from a young woman who cycled through
the raw material, Ojibway and Sioux,
a town confirms, if not a spirit, then
a machinery of compassion, (tab) Q (tab) Return—
and the Carlisle Indian Industrial School
matriculates its share of secretary-clerks
and stellar running backs into a world
at speed, at point, as each and every world
is that ever was: welcome to our pure
forms of forgetting, whole minutes worth, aloft
just above the sands of Kitty Hawk.

Memo: From *The Course of Empire* by Bernard DeVoto

Autumn softens the bluffs on the river
With a haze, and a fierce, finite light—
Rivers flow into other rivers, and they
flow into rivers that flow into the sea.

Imagine, if you will, Coronado's golden city,
for here he stood—never mind the doughnut bakery.
Rivers flow into other rivers, and they
flow into rivers that flow into the sea.

Despite lost tribes of Welshmen,
Ireaelites, Amazons, unicorns, all maps agree:
Rivers flow into other rivers, and they
flow into rivers that flow into the sea.

Why ask the radar on the mountain
for latest news? Here's an update—
Rivers flow into other rivers, and they
flow into rivers that flow into the sea.

You want it when? With graphs and charts?
You give me a headache. I'll give you the summary.
Rivers flow into other rivers, and they
flow into rivers that flow into the sea.

First the diagnosis, then the announcement:
"You're now free to move about the denouement,"
as rivers flow into other rivers, and they
flow into rivers that flow into the sea.

How do I love thee, and why? O congeries
of gorgeous lies, I've lost my way.
And rivers flow into other rivers, and they
flow into rivers that flow into the sea.

THREE
Let Nothing You Dismay

I Recall Being Beautifully Stoned

—Seattle, 1993

In a convertible, with the top down, the wind up,
her hair like the crazy spray of a broken hydrant,
a ghost approached me.

I'd postponed my plan for *Jumping From a Bridge,*
a rambling tract of Death Schtick,
the newest performance craze,
mine to be punctuated by a vault from the rail
of the Aurora Avenue Bridge.

But I'd failed, that day. I didn't jump.

What was left but to work through the jeering crowd?
("He's just a *poseur.* No commitment to the craft.")
& thumb my way home:

She stopped for me, said, "get in," lit a joint, said:
"The perfect BLOW-JOB'S every man's true EL DORADO—
Don't let anyone tell you different."

In a blue print dress, a bad wig,
discreet goatee, fine filaments of reddish arm hair,
it was Pound, of course, who had lobbied,
with qualified success, it seemed, for a variance
on the code of the underworld. He was lecturing already:

"Sheer, shattering PHALLIC impact. THAT'S
what we lived for, BACK IN THE DAY . . ."

He was working on a wad of Beechnut
packed into his lower lip. He reached for a cup,
spat, set it down, began waving his hands like a conductor

—"YR all either jumping off bridges," a pause, for my sake,
or waiting for the NEXT BIG THING"—

eyes asquint, searching the rear view mirror,
the disappointed crowd behind us thinning out—

"Whatever the HELL *that* was suppose to be,"
Then, an evaluative glance—"How's your Latin?"

In a car driven by the great ghost of Pound
with wild hair and tobacco stains on his dress,
the look in his eye was fierce, but fearful, too,
my silence a dread confirmation,
I sank like an object dropped from a height.

"Well, anyhow, 'twas seldom *spoken,* if at all, actually,"
his voice trailing off.

We fell silent, both of us absorbed,
in a hempish sort of way,
into the summer stream of evening traffic purring
all around us down the gaudy thoroughfare
of Aurora—

        "The Renaissance INVENTED perspective,"
Pound blurted out, a propos of nothing,

"the technique of DEPTH and DISTANCE,

"the vanishing point, smuggled in someone's pocket
like a tomato seedling across the waters,

"and this grew into something we wanted
to vanish into:
      cf. Boone into Kentucky,
          Colter, down the Yellowstone . . ."

And here, too, as far as one could see,
the vanishing had neither flagged nor faltered—
Coronado's banners and whirly-gigs fluttered over
cars and discount furniture stores
and streets where people waited
between having and getting.

And as far as one could see,
          one could get
an oil change, a back rubbed,
          or have
the world's shortest little nervous breakdown
before the light turned green.

And as far as one could see,
the speed limit in Purgatory was a steady
five over the posted 40, so we kept apace,
and we stopped when they stopped, and looked
straight ahead, as they looked straight ahead.

And we said nothing, as they said nothing—
and our souls, such as they were, CAR-RT sorted,
settled and idling in unison, murmured
a catchy, toe-tapping, panicked little song.

—"What is this place?" Pound said, at last.
—"North 85th and Greenwood," I said, helpfully.

—"No, no," with a sweep of his hand
that took in the Piggly Wiggly & the strip northward
                              clear to Canada
—"No," he said again. "I mean, THIS!?"

The White Pages

You'll find him listed under King, as in—
Kong, brought back in chains,
           Kong on tour with Ringling Bros.
see also: colossal metaphor, projected fear,
reading Marcus Garvey and Du Bois.

Photos on the wall: the early years—
Kong in love, that boyish thatch of hair,
           Kong awry, gone off with our young Miss.
Terrible, lusting, big-fingered Kong,
crushed, bereft, knowing it's all wrong—

Knowing, up there, in a strafing wind,
there's no real pleasure swatting planes,
           bashing cars. It hurts to be writ large.
(Yet, whom shall we send, who can handle this?)
Who would have known! Who would have guessed?

Kong!, with tasseled shoes, big cigars!
Ironic Kong, media king conglomerate,
           on tour with his Tachikawa stars,
in deep now for money and for points—decisions:
Godzilla, again, or *The Thing From Mars?*

Kong on the phone, saying "Yes, this is Kong.
Fine, and you?" Kong alone in mid-town bars.
           Put it on his tab. He's good for it.
And, anyway, who'd refuse?
Who'd say, I'm sorry, you've had enough, Kong?

Lean years stranded with the motivational
a cappella choir "Up With People!"
           Talk about awkward. All those bright-eyed
smiles and flailing elbows, and in the back,
in gold medallions and polyester Sans-a-belt slacks,

Kong! hitting the low notes, casting long
shadows over prairie towns
    in Decatur, Illinois, Willamette, Oregon—
a silhouette over malls outside Spokane,
Kong, let's face it—We love you, man.

Minimalism

—*after* Empire, *a film by Andy Warhol*

—the small

                  begets the large,

       the part

the whole;

       and nothing's nothing less than

       something's other—

And this just in—stop the presses, call
the National Guard—

words are nothing more than

                a rattled mechanism, multiplied

     in scape, in scope—an empire held,

     both far and near,

in departments of interior—

(for the latest dispatch from the front,
simply check the mirror). *Ho hum*

Kong, in tedium, figures here, too, finally,

as a fool goes forth in has-been-hood,

                acting out of habit, or of love,

     like a backward looking

weekend skater on the Pond.

But let's face it, Graceful Kong, it's
out with the old, in with the smooth

              Apollonian,

     glitterings of the mind—

     so that: the least

that we can do arrives, like larceny,
makes us sad, here, at the end of the line.

And eight hours takes some time.
    The film sets us dead against
    our dear old friend,
        see *stream* or *flow of*—
takes its measure, says behold,
like a certain taste for the lash and cord,

this course (as in Empire, see also, State)
                    this premise of yours,
        this river we've heard so much about,
        flickers through the teeth and gears,
this winged fugitive and all of that . . .
he of the wan lasso, and with one or two assistants,

a factory of hangers on,
has brought to a bunkered, pile-driven stop
                a building, like a stolen prima mobile.
        Watch it if you will, but it's no use no good
        you won't last—
but an hour, at most two—
but it will measure you   an ocean, cup

by tiny cup, frame by frame—

        too big to take in
                    says the door man. *Too tall to tell*
        says Super Man, *too long to know*
        says Attention Deficit Disorder Man—
at fifty-seven thousand frames an hour.
What is that—some kind of a joke?,
        (Kong, yelling from the back)

Well, yeah, but don't expect a pause,
                a rest, a rope, a ring, a towel, a bell,
        some late-phase referee to step in,
        some book-ish life guard to toss us,
from the safety of the shore, an ellipsis,
a gap to give some breathing room

for the gist, the general idea, to be happy in—
No.

Pre-Amputee To Reviewers

You are like the surgeon who operates
on the wrong leg.

I sit up on the gurney
and with a magic marker,
in ink that won't wash off,
I write this note for you
on the good leg—the one you are not to touch:

Dear Doctor,

This is the wrong leg.
Please move over to the other leg.
But wait: why, bent to your
terrible task, are you reading this
in the first place?

Catastrophilia: As If Written Somewhere, Say, At A Place Unknown, And, Perhaps, Never To Be Known (To Ambrose Bierce)

As to me, I leave here tomorrow for an unknown destination.
—Bierce's last known communication, December, 26, 1913

Everyone's looked for you in Mexico,
or, to the north, in the West Texas scrub
some graveyard the wind and sand erased
    to nub
     & thorn
the wind a kind of lovely,
        emergency music
broadcast, tonight
in the oak antennae clicking in the wind—
in the single cone of light,
scuttling along the ocean floor
     of Nevada—

in the backscatter of stars, migrating eels,
the endless nod tuned to God,

whole civilizations having risen, vanished,
declared themselves again under the ancient
star-light of the plains—

No grave, then, no convenient spot to ponder,
no setting, no quarry found,
     just a quandary—

just the gleaming premise
of Walker Percy Chrysler,
    in chromium,
in a blind chrysalis, a sun-torched flare

of Empire, shining with a power and a glory,
in fugue, (Gold to Silver, Silver to Bronze)
                    —just the fusillade
of city buildings assembled and gathered

over the orchestral blat of horns magnificent,
persons and titles important, who maketh
                        not a thing on earth
but add to the pitch
                their own shifty weight in fine cigars—

—only a sweet rumbling overhead,
over tenements and the hall of echos,
smashed glass and staccato
                            counterpoint
of semi-automatic weapon's fire

—the singing bride
                of the fireball,
the soft whistling of someone stepping
                        casually into the crosshairs

—for the Zoans and Ephesians are at it again,
                        as is their wont,
and the Nophs are deceived in the bulrushes,
and the Twelve Tribes of Israel want a snack—

                something to tide them over the onset
                of the in-coming,

something to wail once the whelming commences,
someone to render the sundering—

on the Jericho Turnpike,
traffic stacked up from Heshbon to Nimrim

—It's not the wreckage, only the actual,

oncoming wreck itself,
Ladies, Gentlemen; Friends, Romans—

are you with me?

—all the personal poets of America
toughing it out like old Boethius in his cell,

out of favor
with some Ostrogoth or other, 524 AD
darkness closing on the City of Man. . . .

—◇◇◇—

How strange to have seen the momentum of empire shift
into overdrive—*God invented war,* you wrote,
to teach American's geography.
You're right here,
of course,
though your bones were never found.

The Alleghenies this time of year,
befogged in patches,
are good for ghosting, don't ask me how I know.

I just do. It's no great trick. I'm half-dead already.
And that's half of what joins us two.

Just glad to have found you, sir, finally,
though where *that* is, of course, I haven't said,
& won't, other than to offer the kind of hint
that gives it all away: if you want a secret kept,
hide it in a book of poems.

Glib:

1) Not far from *glob,* and *globule,*
in *Web II,* akin to *glissade,* as in slippery, a skillful slide,
a way of going about one's life, perhaps? You won't find *glib,*
anyhow, as an entry in Mr. Bierce's dictionary,
for it must have seemed self-evident, like *breath,*
which also goes undefined. *Breath,* by the way, would have fit
between *brain, v.t. to rebuke bluntly . . .*
to dispel a source of error in an opponent—
(as in, the pieces of a cane with which Bierce once *brained*
a former associate, for example, & which he saved
to remind himself of the nature of friendship)
—and *Brandy, n. a cordial composed of one part thunder-and-lightning,*
one part remorse. . . . Dose: a headful all the time.

        & with said headful,

Bierce, bent over Gibbon's *Decline and Fall,*
became "Bierce," "A.G.," a third person, a sleek familiar,
such that *glib* grew as a wound
around a blade. No word for that, either.
You just embody it.

2) Glib: wit under the weather, (i.e, drunk);
the occupational hazard
of one burdened with being,
(i.e., drunk) in weekly installments.

Tho sometimes it turned out rather well, *cf Reliquary, n. A receptacle*
for such sacred objects as pieces of the true cross,
short-ribs of the saints . . .
                the head of Saint Dennis,
which, because of misbehavior in Canterbury cathedral
(it, the head, was searching—rather loudly—for a body of doctrine)
was *thrown into the Stour.*

3) a habit of mind borne of the long view,
e.g., bent over Gibbon's *Decline and Fall.*
To a lady author hectoring him for advice from the ancients
on the rearing of the young:

Study Herod, madam—study Herod.

4) An all together too easy tactic or strategy, it seems, issued from some great remove—

4) e.g., God's view of the predicament

4) Ha!

4)—if, indeed, God had anything to do with it:
note the brows arching over eyes set too close together,
the neck thrust forward,
in a rare and deadly combination of ferocity and perplexity,
fingers gripping the podium of empire,
behind which lie hidden the duct-tape,
boom mics and cameras of empire—the shutter-flash like a thousand
cicadas—or like laughter

5) as one of three condemned soldiers for the Union Army
whose hanging Bierce oversaw,
shouted from the gallows, *I'm coming, Jesus!*
and as if on cue,
a locomotive whistle blew
a long, derisive hoot—
& the assembled crowd of officers and enlisted
burst into it, a rolling laughter
which the condemned must have heard,
Bierce reminds us,
as they dropped into the hereafter

6) Used in a sentence: *the glib laughter less mirthful
perhaps, than the product of a habitual grimace*

7) Glib: a place of refuge that becomes a trap,

8) an unwitting concession, a way of being a ghost.

Memo: to Bierce, Crossing the Mississippi

Fuck it all—I'd say we'd better let the dead
fend for themselves. This is seconded,
in the calm drift of the figurative,
by the slumber of dogs, &c, who lie, or is it *lay?*
The soul, in any case, being transitive,
wants a crossing—never mind where to,
though that, I'm afraid, keeps seeping through,
keeps dawning on them, as it must have,
surely, on any given bright & shining day.
Tell me, what was it you once believed?
What exception to the general rule,
what clause, what special instance, were you?
Here, hope against hope, rage against rage
begins. Just look. Just lift your eyes from the page.

Empire Burlesque

The president is pacing in his room—
Order out, order in? Snowfall clobbers the capital.
There is no kingdom in our kingdom of the moon.

All things to all and everyone—
O, my fever dream, my translucent girl . . .
The president is pacing in his room.

Troubles mount and shift, of course, and soon
Amid the drift we'll sound like keening spaniels—
"There's no *kingdom* in our kingdom of the moon."

Friends, Romans . . . embrace the chain of command,
eternity . . . whatever's left—a sky like mother-of-pearl,
a president pacing in his room.

The storm unleashed, the Pope on hold, an idea come—
"Quick, get a pencil." "Sir?" . . . He scribbles
All there is—*no kingdom in our kingdom of the moon . . .*

And the rest, that brilliant, ferocious question
Beneath a sky like hammered steel? No matter.
The president is pacing in his room.
There is no kingdom in our kingdom of the moon.

FOUR
News to Pluto

News to Pluto

Do not, under any circumstances, bring up
The Chuck Berry Sex Video, for instance,
the news of which will never reach Pluto, one prays.
It may be true they've assigned undue
reverence for certain cultural ejecta (their hymns
are based on a Rick Wakeman solo project, it seems)
but when they point backward along the asymptote
through ice and dark matter to that speck of star as tiny as a nit,
our signal flailing against the noise,
and say, *Maybe something interesting's happen there!*
just know there's not enough gravity on Pluto
to hold more than one meaning at once, let alone its opposite.
Your irony is out their window. Tread lightly, in other words.
They really want to know.

                    And when, from your
great remove, and with a few dozen mouse-clicks,
you zoom in like a god, right down to their rooftops,
(at such proximity the resolution goes to shit,
& things begin to blur and get downright blobular),
the trick, then, of course is to jettison the fancy gadgetry
and hand the craft over to a poem

                  a door clicks
quietly, at one AM, the engine cut—
the sound of tires rolling on gravel to a stop,
(drogue chutes drifting through the pines
like hushed voices),
your eyes adjusting to the light

                        of Pluto,

                  when you land,
again, (and here's the thing: it's never the first time)
you do so, not because it's right
or good, or because you hope to make amends,
or resolve a grudge or two,

or, in a weak moment, imagine that you've come
to deliver the celebrity commencement address
long overdue but finally bestowed,
nor have you come, as you start to hope,
looking down your derelict block,
because of some colossal administrative error, say,
some spectacularly maladroit transposition
of destinations (e.g. for Paris, Pluto).
On this point, I've got no lesson for you.
You're here, as it starts to sink in (again)
for reasons that simply don't apply
anywhere, which is the guiding prerogative
of a darkened and now decommissioned planet.
And it's not your place to tell them what you've heard.
The news to Pluto will arrive soon enough
and won't be what they don't already know.

Helen, the Extra Special

whose face launched a thousand cruise ships—

a thousand trailer caravans
deep into the subdivided heart of the Havermeyers

and the Jaycees and the Finsters and the Prelowitz's,
a thousand versions of the Prelowitz's,

who took their journey from Saginaw
encamped in Yuma, Arizona, Moab, Utah—

amid chaparral, and creosote and wolf bush,
the knuckled hills and draws of,

the fanned & feathered, blasted glass of
White Sands Missile Range,

The Red River Valley, and
                    On Top of Old Smokey—
who ask of the ciphering wind

        When, O, when—

She of the Golden Girls Lady Golfers,
Addresses the ball on the fourteenth tee,

in a sun hat, in a garden full of rocks—
she of the many-colored coo-coo clocks,

wind mills, wind chimes, wind socks—
who floats entire industries thereof

of table coasters and matching ashtray sets,
and clam-shell orchestras,

She, the Very Right Honorable Mrs. He
of He fame, the late he himself,

who went whole-hog on her, then died—
she who hit the trail, which ended here,

rips a shot over scorched alluvial flats,
over Bermuda grass, shaped and trimmed

like so many greening kidneys
framed by glands of bunker sand,

she whose clocks are always wound,
whose sons, scattered with the wind,

observe us from their places
with the perfect, retouched faces
of the dead—
she whose smile that always said:

> *Are We Having Fun Yet?*
She'd really rather be in Authentic City—

authentic cowboys, authentic cats.
Authentic clowns in paper hats.

Authentic mountains, authentic lakes.
Authentic clouds, authentic fakes.

An authentic breeze luffs the sail,
parts the hair on your authentic head.

Your life you live authentically,
Your death you die, authentic, dead.

Call us now. We're standing by
Take a left at the revival tent,
                   then a right at the sky.

—◄◆►—

At night, from desert mountain tops
horripilating with antennae—

with the proper alignment—
you can see the flight pattern of in-coming jets,

a terraced, ziggurat descending
from some top-most tier of atmosphere,

from St. Cloud, from Rockland,
from Chandeleur Island, from Peoria

by way of Kuybyshev and Sverdlovsk,
Phan Rang and Mindanao . . .

arriving, as it were, for the full buffet
we've heard so much about—

She, the cause of all this blather,
awakens from her nap, the in-flight movie over,

adjusts her seat back, tray and table,
the flight attendants cross check

and strap down as they all nose in—
the roaring, paint-blistering

ball of fire over desert palms—
(the unlikely event) is calmly shelved again,

as the swelling, signifying shadow of a plane
and the plane itself, converge, touch the earth.

Catastrophilia

Once, so drunk I spoke spontaneous Danish—
in an ecstasy, I baffled our arresting officer,
who pardoned me in his best Iowan, and sent us
down the road. For it had come to this,
sweet exile and an occasional citation for
public exposure, and Tuesday Night Euchre,
which I'd grown to love I must confess.
That, and the lovely, the fatal, Olga Skuladottir,
quick-fingered artist stranded there
in the heartland, laconic shuffler of cards and men,
praying for tornadoes, whose sirens flared
over hilltops, it seemed, as dawn approached,
& dimmed as we'd descend to our disaster stations
of painted cinder block, naked & far from God.

Brodsky, Seattle, 1984

Chance brought me near, a clean traffic record,
a car, a friend who called—*He's in town.*
Do you want to, like, chauffeur him around?
Thus was a fool struck dumb and blind
by his brush with the historical, who threw us off guard—
"What rhymes with *Toyota?*" He paused (I groan
remembering) and made *us* feel at home.
—*iota?* he offered, helpfully. I was terrified.
I'd picked the place: white linen, table lamps.
He smoked, told toilet jokes from the camps,
said nothing of our ignorance of Seneca and Donne.
Ours was a free fall he'd grown into, an abyss
he'd summon like a waiter, then dismiss,
laughing—for there was nothing beneath him.

Moon Too Easy After Bone

You with your straw-colored hair all
ablaze: *like a pit boss in a torrid zone*
someone said—*No, more like Sting on Soul
Cages,* composing songs for the noumenon.

You smelled of feral goat and gun metal,
Drum tobacco—pronounced to rhyme with *gloom*—
Pointing to the evening star, which clicked on,
you'd ask "Who's got a joke for me?" We'd look down,

panicked, silent, scuffing gravel, kicking marl,
bone white under the moon—
"No, no, no!" you'd yell, later; "Moon's
too easy after bone. Why not *Novicain,* or *vibraphone?*"

Later, aimiably stewed in an adirondack chair—
by the way, darling, I don't have straw-colored hair.

Orpheus, Pt. Townsend, Washington

Mornings on the beach, magisterially early,
you'd been up for hours while we'd lumbered,
yea, verily, clear-cutting the forests of Siberia,
soon to be hung-over, disabled & bound

by a sense of yet another capitulation
to cliché: *should I leave my diaphragm in?*
Stumped, as it were, I sprang for the strange.
I labored for nearly an *hour* over a poem.

By then you'd come up from the shore,
as sails unfurled over the glint of the sound.
A woman out of R. Crumb cut across the field,
all breasts and boots and calves. You stared at her

then read my poem: "Krakatoa Toothbrush Painters."
Strange, you said, *but predictable, like yesterday's antlers.*

Catastrophilia: The High Concept

Oceans Rise. Cities Fall. Hope Survives.

Hearts break. Time flies.
Meteorite Flattens Metropolis.

> Pigs Fly (On Dare)
> so that:

Love calls. Duty calls.
Molten lava engulfs orphanage.

> Buster Keaton meets Issac Newton
> Issak Walton meets Walter Benjamin

Thomas Jefferson meets The Blob
meets Captain Kirk meeting Kitty Carlisle

> Kahil Gibran meets Fog Horn Leg Horn
> meets Madonna meeting Donna Reed

as Sacagawea meeting Kali
opening for George Thoroughgood & the Destroyers.

Li Po meets Truman Capote
meeting Edgar Allan Poe meeting Pocahontas for drinks.

—◆◇◆—

> (A series
>   of twists and turns,
>   meets
>   a mini-series
>   of twists and turns)

Long Time Traveling Here Below

For Molly Tenenbaum

Tell my love the life-like
run through thus to halts,
a fist upon the hip, with her—

tell her then begins the shuck
and ratchet music, the gearworks
& levers, the whole shebang—

telephone tonight and dwell
upon the canticle's
pretty good trick—

the hibernal, then the sash
of summer, float bugs on the water,
cottonwoods—she'll say:

better level the reveler
than talk about the dew point
and the cider, and the field

with the fog in it—
cattails lopped haphazard
and a donkey's racket

down in the swale—
humor her—whack the carpet,
toss the dust puppets,

harvest the hokum,
crack the window open—
slap the happy—

wear the juju necklace
and watch the cat watch
the weaver bird

scat the old song
across the lot, (two oaks
in full leaf)—

and the hiccup
hieroglyph
woven into thickets.

—◇◇◇—

Could it be they've entered it, a signature,
a signal, demarking an extent, another limit

to beguile a 'limitless supply,'
despite her bad elbow, which burns as they play?

Though assiduous with the ice
she keeps hoping the trouble away

with good whiskey and candles,
and the smaller flames of *Buffalo Gals,*

and *Five to My Five,* and *Sweet Afton.*
—or could it be what the empty air's become

when you're not around fiddle music
anymore, but think you're still hearing some?

—◇◇◇—

Molly T. and her *Band o' Lyres,* for instance,
hot-footing it to make the last ferry
past Poulsbo in the smoking Datsun, 3AM,
the trunk-latch broken and back seat
piled to the mirrors with patch cords & mandolins,
and Bill the Bass w/his O-ring mouth
mussing up the window vent.

Soon everyone and her brother will look out
for the shape and tenor of the day—
high overcast, gauzed with blue. . . .
                              you wanted something else?

For now the moon shoulders through the scrim.
They make passage in a darkness
smelling of new paint and bunker fuel,
wedged between an Alpha Romeo &
an Omega Farms egg truck. Bill yawns,

settles deep into his creaking leather coat.
The ferry churns for Elliott slip
                    & they sleep
like monks to thrumming, demon-like drums.

To an Unknown Poet, Dead at 39

—Phil Perelson, 1956—1995

Love, it seems, when all is said and done,
Kept you (maintained, withheld) indefinite.
In bits and pieces you offered your *Te Deum.*

To disappear was your "natural condition,"
but what to keep (guard, record) against the infinite,
when love, it seems, when all is said and done,

(so utter, complete) so obliterates someone?
Your "Five Keys to Anonymity," the ball & chain habits?
In bits and pieces you offered your *Te Deum.*

I still say "you," a mistake I see, for the third person
holds you (faithful, spellbound now) separate—
Love it seems, when all is said and done,

Need not answer back, or get a word in
Edgewise, or feel at all compelled to speculate
In bits and pieces. You offered your *Te Deum,*

and what remains? What space along what margin,
what wisp in a rented room, what scrap, however delicate?
Love, it seems, when all is said and done.
In bits and pieces, you offered your *Te Deum.*

Memo on the Sublime: To Longinus from San Francisco

Oblivion: Cold storage for high hopes.

About you we know next to nothing,
your name, for instance. A wind blows through my window.
It scatters the papers on my desk while in the kitchen
I'm making salad with anchovies, which would disgust
my wife, but she's not here, and so—*Maestro, Please*—
a little song, if you will, for this much maligned species:
If I were a dog, I would roll in you,
and rock the dog world.

—your name, which anchors you against the general scattering
was, of course, a monk's guess, some anonymous someone's
inspired moment—in a darkened room, tallow burning in a corner.
He was out all day, fishing, when a storm blew in,
his skin feeling tight from sun and salt air,
and now he's alone and happy with, I like to think,
a plate of grilled anchovies, beside which lies
the unpromising moth-eaten treatise in rhetoric
for ambitious young Romans—
                    which says, oddly for a primer,
                    what I want to tell you can't be taught.

After lunch I pedal into the Marina, the Presidio,
climbing the switchback where the breakers
hit the rocks, the traffic roaring above,
then I'm on the bridge, passing the southern tower
then the span and you're so high you've simply left
the sound of the waters below.
Gone are the sounds of the world also
                    of bells and distant trains
                    the clinking of silverware

Up here it's just you
and the rust-colored vaulted into blue
colossi of the gods, if they're real,
and you don't know they're not,

not here, anyway, where they make a pretty hard case for themselves,
though it's we of course who ascended mightily
once and here's a bridge

                    as proof—
                    and it's we,

who strangely drive our cars above the clouds
as if it were the commonest thing in the world.
Dear World: I am getting along okay. Today
I will have a snack in Sausalito, then bicycle back
downtown, where I am staying in a little boutique hotel
I don't have to pay for. I will jump off the street car
like a pro and go upstairs for a hot bath, so, you know,
to answer Camus' question, which comes to mind now,
& which I read as an undergrad, deeply
impressed, but also wondering if Camus weren't
just a wee bit of a light-weight, compared to, say, Sartre,
but look how time has dealt with Sartre—*eh, Camus?!*—
—whether to kill oneself or to go on living
was, in fact, the one philosophical question, as Camus says.
Well, I can't complain, which means, like these
commuters motoring on their asses through the empyrean,
most of the time, alas, I suppose I'm neither dead nor alive.

Others, in numbers enough
to make this a bridge into the hereafter, have paused,
then leapt over the rails,
notes folded, placed in ziplock bags,
or attached to clothing, perhaps with safety pins—

Survival of the fittest, Adios—Unfit.

Absolutely no reason except I have a toothache.

As for me, I would have gone on a bit, I tend to go on,
I do go on, so it seems,
across a bridge that blows me sideways
though one wonders, at times, where to,
as if there were some doubt in the matter,

the afternoon light glorious, O gods,
and of course one's fate is to be less than misremembered.

Notes

Empire Burlesque, the title of this book, occurred to me in 1996, as I was finishing *Soul Data* and embarking upon my next project. This was before Ken Burns got a hold of Lewis and Clark but not before Stephen Ambrose did, whose *Undaunted Courage* set in motion a project that I did not know would take me ten years to complete, Lewis and Clark and others—Kong, Pound, Bierce—patiently waiting by the river bank as other things marvelously intervened, way leading on to way, and the years amassed. I did not know of the eponymous Bob Dylan album until late in the game when someone pointed this out. *Dylan,* I thought. *Of course.* You won't find him here, unless the large things that shape us remain, like back-scatter in the cosmos, both nowhere and everywhere. For truth-in-labeling purposes, I requisitioned a poem from *Soul Data,* confusingly titled "Empire Burlesque," from a warehouse in Denton, Texas, and put it on page 56, where it sits recuperating. If you have gotten to this point looking for *Empire Burlesque: High Crimes and Low Comedy in the Bush Administration,* well, congratulations. This is not that book.

"Memo: Understanding As I Do That This Little Work Would be Nothing In Itself . . . etc, etc" (p. 1). The longish title, taken directly from Pedro de Castaneda's preface to *The Journey of Coronado,* amused me.

Plus Ultra ("You Can Go Beyond"; section title p. 5). Charles V's motto, conceived circa 1516.

"Jeffersonian," (pp. 7–13). "Yonder star-swirl might compose/but the smallest flower or leaf thereof": David Rittenhouse's speculation, correct, as it turns out, about galaxies in the universe. Rittenhouse, one of Jefferson's circle, along with Benjamin Rush, lampooned in this poem, Joseph Priestly, Thomas Paine, and Charles Wilson Peale, built an Orrery that, according to Daniel J. Boorstin's *The Lost World of Thomas Jefferson,* was "considered the first mechanical wonder of the American world." Other quotes are from Thomas Jefferson's instructions to Lewis and Clark and from the laundry list of articles brought on the expedition as found in *The Journals of Lewis and Clark.* The following excerpts were found in the fabulous and strangely moving *Myth of the West: America as the Last Empire,* by Jan Willem Schulte Nordholt: *The ocean breaks its shackles / and a great earth lies open . . .* is from Seneca's *Medea; Tunc Orientis occidit et ortum est Occidentis imperium,* [when the might of the East declined, that of the West arose], is from Orosius, pupil of Augustine, in his history of the world; "and a new generation ascends . . . *imperium sine fine dedi*" [an empire that will never end], is from Virgil's fourth eclogue.

"*Exeunt*" (p. 17). Playing fast and loose as this volume does with *The Journals of Lewis and Clark,* I recall a mention of migrating squirrels, so I had them thundering through the treetops. The rest is invention.

"Memo from the Platte" (p. 18). *Caught 500 catfish near the river mouth . . .* For concision, I may have rounded-up the actual number. I don't know about you, but that's a lot of catfish.

"Voyager, 1804" (p. 19). Labiche's fantasy is not in *The Journals,* of course, but the notation for latitude and longitude are, so X marks the spot where someone yearned.

"Memo: As the State of Mind in Which We Are, Generally, Gives the Colouring To Events, When The Imagination is Suffered to Wander Into Futurity" (21). So much of interior life goes unsaid in *The Journals,* or gets glossed with the much-used, throw-away phrase "& etc," which deserves its own poem, that this title, which comes from one of Lewis' entries, struck me as a rare moment of disclosure, almost a premonition. During a long winter with the Mandans, Joe Shields was able to trade food for sheet iron from a forge he'd constructed. The first volumes of *The Journals,* published years after Lewis' probable suicide, included passages describing the incantatory sexual rituals meant to draw buffalo closer to the Indian encampment, the more explicit passages of which were chastely translated into Latin by Nicholas Biddle.

"VI Shannon, Lost" (p. 29). Shannon, the youngest member of the Corps of Discovery, gets lost. Days later, John Colter finds him. I'm interested in the way mistaken assumptions acquire the force of destiny. Here Shannon assumes, mistakenly, that he's been passed, or left behind, when in fact, he is traveling *in front* of the Corps. His daily effort to "catch up," which only widens the distance between them, feels like a parable.

"The Past as Obsolete Gesture" (p. 36). Marianne Moore taught business English to the pupils of The Carlisle Indian Industrial School (Now the United States Army War College) where founder and former Indian fighter Richard Henry Pratt hoped to assimilate Ojibway, Sioux, and other boarding-school-age tribal members by teaching them how to type ("Tab Q tab return"), etc. The school's football team, coached by Glenn "Pop" Warner, invented the forward pass, among other things, and included Hall of Fame running back Jim Thorpe, whose career Moore followed throughout her life.

"The White Pages" (p. 44). His car found abandoned by the Golden Gate Bridge, God bless you, Weldon Kees.

"Pre-Amputee to Reviewers" (p. 49). This poem is an adaptation for my own purposes of a joke I heard performed at a benefit for the Bronx Academy of Letters.

"News to Pluto" (p. 59). A Rick Wakeman solo project? The joke is lost if I have to explain, alas—too bad for me. It's unclear if the poem itself is improved by reading it while listening to the keyboard player for the prog rock group *Yes*'s *Journey to the Centre of the Earth,* but you are welcome to try. Attention insomniacs: possibly a first use of Google Earth as a guiding image in an American poem?

"Long Time Traveling Here Below" (p. 69). "Molly T. and her Band o' Lyres"—the name of an old-time music group which, if it doesn't exist, should.

"Memo on the Sublime: To Longinus from San Francisco" (p. 73). The epigraph is from San Francisco resident provocateur, Ambrose Bierce. For more on Longinus and the Sublime see Glenn W. Most, "After the Sublime," *The Yale Review,* vol. 90, no 2 (April 2002) or Mark Svenvold, *Big Weather: Chasing Tornadoes in the Heart of America,* Henry Holt & Co, pp. 92–105.